WORLD FOLKTALES

A Multicultural Approach to Whole Language

GRADES K–2

By Jerry Mallett
and
Keith Polette

Alleyside Press
Fort Atkinson, Wisconsin

Published by Alleyside Press, an imprint of Highsmith Press
Highsmith Press
W5527 Highway 106
P.O. Box 800
Fort Atkinson, Wisconsin 53538-0800

1-800-558-2110

© Jerry Mallett and Keith Polette, 1994
Cover design: Frank Neu

The paper used in this publication meets the minimum requirements of
American National Standard for Information Science —
Permanence of Paper for Printed Library Material. ANSI/NISO Z39.48-1992.

Library of Congress Cataloging in Publication
  Mallet, Jerry J., 1939-
    World folktales : a multicultural approach to whole language /
  by Jerry Mallett and Keith Polette.
      p.   cm.
  Includes bibliographical references.
  Contents: [1] K-2 -- [2] 3-5 -- [3] 6-8.
  ISBN 0-917846-43-5 (v. 1 : alk. paper). --ISBN 0-917846-44-3
  (v. 2 : alk. paper). -- ISBN 0-917846-45-1 (v. 3 : alk. paper)
  1. Tales--Study and teaching (Elementary)--United States.
  2. Language experience approach in education--United States.
  3. Multicultural education--United States.
  I. Polette, Keith, 1954-   . II. Title.
  LB1576.M3625 1994
    372.64--dc20   94-21691

CONTENTS

INTRODUCTION

This book is based upon the premise that children learn most effectively and efficiently by becoming active participants in the process of education. Quite simply, this means that children learn least when they sit passively for hours and read and respond to material in which they are not both mentally and emotionally engaged. One approach which allows and encourages children to become more involved in learning is Whole Language. Whole Language is not a system, or a specific set of strategies, but is rather a different kind of educational orientation which places the student at the center of the learning situation. Consequently, Whole Language relies heavily upon the perceptions and experiences that the student brings to the classroom every day because these experiences are the base upon which Whole Language is built.

The activities in *World Folktales: A Multicultural Approach to Whole Language*, are designed to help the teacher create a Whole Language environment by using the experiences of the student as a bridge to increased literacy through active involvement. In addition, the activities are holistic in format, being based as they are upon a multiplicity of both productive and critical (higher order) thinking skills, which means that the whole student, not just an isolated part of his/her brain, will be engaged in learning.

The specific educational objectives of this book are for the student to: gain an appreciation for folktales as a literary genre; gain an increased understanding and appreciation of world cultures as expressed through their various folktales; demonstrate high order thinking processes with increased facility; acquire a higher level of literacy; develop more efficient writing, speaking and listening skills; develop the ability to respond to a literary text in a myriad of clear and purposeful ways; develop more sophisticated language patterns; and develop a strong working vocabulary.

The activities in this book are ready to be used in the language arts classroom without requiring a great deal of preparation time. Many are also designed to be enjoyable, to take the malaise that many students feel out of learning. Consequently, this book will help the teacher create a strong sense of "psychological safety" in the classroom. When students feel "safe," that is, when they feel that their experiences, perceptions and ideas are valid and acceptable, they will often see more purpose for reading, writing, speaking, listening and thinking in the classroom. The Whole Language approach allows the teacher to become more of a facilitator and to also make his/her job easier and more rewarding. When both the students and the teacher are relaxed, true learning begins.

BOOK ORGANIZATION

For easy use and clarity, *World Folktales: A Multicultural Approach to Whole Language* is arranged into the following eight cultural units:

African American/Africa (Sukuma Tribe)

Middle East/India (Turkey)

Jewish/Yiddish

Asian (Vietnam)

Native American/Inuit (Cherokee)

East European (Russia)

West European (Norway)

Hispanic (Mexico)

These eight cultural sections are organized into uniform units. Each unit begins with a folktale indigenous to that particular cultural group. This is followed by three activity sections emphasizing the Whole-Language approach: Before Reading Activities, During Reading Activities and After Reading Activities. Each unit is completed with student activity sheets which may be copied for immediate student use.

A "Story Integration" section may be found at the end of the book. This section is composed of Whole-Language activities which overlap and combine all of the folktales found here.

HOW FROG LOST HIS TAIL

FOLKTALE FROM AFRICA — SUKUMA TRIBE

Frog lived on the edge of a water hole. His home was the muddy bank. He was unhappy because he knew he did not like to see his reflection in the water. Instead of a big mouth that looked like a dark empty cave, he wished for a small fine mouth. Instead of two eyes that looked like silly doorknobs, he wished for soft and beautiful eyes. But what he wished for more than anything in the world was a long handsome tail.

Each day at sundown when the forest and savanna animals came to drink, they swished their tails and teased poor Frog. "Look at Frog squatting on the bank. He doesn't have a tail," they would laugh.

Frog was so unhappy he went to Nyankonpon, the Sky God. Nyankonpon said to Frog, "What do you want?"

Frog answered, "I want you to make all the animals at the pond stop laughing at me."

And Nyankonpon asked, "How?"

"Make me as strong as Elephant, as swift as Leopard, as graceful as Gazelle and as wise as Eagle."

Nyankonpon said, "That I cannot do. You are a frog and you must remain a frog."

Frog looked up to Nyankonpon and cried, "Couldn't I at least have a tail. That is all I really want."

"Very well," said the Sky God. "I will give you a tail if you promise to guard my magic pond that never dries up."

"I will guard it with my life," said Frog. "But first my tail!"

And the Sky God granted Frog his wish.

The next day when the other animals came to drink from the magic pond, Frog swished his new tail in their faces and drove them all away. Frog croaked at them, "Go away! The Sky God and I do not want you here. There is only room at this pond for me and my beautiful new tail."

The animals were startled.

"What!" trumpeted Elephant.

"Nonsense!" snorted Gazelle.

"Ridiculous!" growled Leopard.

"Unbelievable!" shrieked Eagle.

The animals caused such a commotion that they awakened Nyankonpon, who was napping in the clouds. "What is all this commotion at my magic pond?" he called in his most powerful voice.

Standing at the edge of the magic pond Nyankonpon said to Frog, "What are you doing?"

"I am guarding this pond. *My* pond. And if you know what's good for you, you better go away or I will trounce you with my tail."

The Sky God stood very still, then he shook with anger. Lightning flashed in his eyes. He said to Frog, "You have gone too far. You have forgotten your promise. Therefore, I must take back your tail."

Thunder crashed over the pond and when all was quiet, Frog had no tail.

But the Sky God did not stop there. He found a way to remind Frog of how terrible he acted when he had a tail. Every spring time when new frogs are born as tadpoles, they have long beautiful tails. But as the tadpoles grow and become frogs their beautiful tails shrink and disappear. And that is how Frog lost his tail.

Whole-Language Activities for "How Frog Lost His Tail"

Before Reading Activities

Attentive listening / Chalk talk

1. Tell the children the following story prior to reading "How Frog Lost His Tail." Simply draw the lines shown below in the story as you tell it.

2. After the telling, ask the children what you drew on the board. Yes, a frog.

3. Now list some of the words they can remember from your telling of the story, such as, savannah, forest, water hole, animals, etc. Review this list asking the children which words they think will be in the story "How Frog Lost His Tail."

Who Saved the Animals?

A very long time ago in Africa…

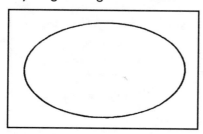

the animals lived in two groups. One group lived in the savannah…

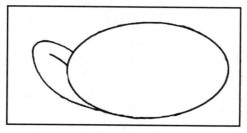

…the other group lived in the forest.

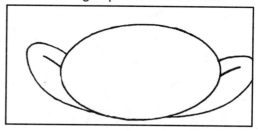

Both groups of animals got along very nicely and rarely was there a fight or even an argument. In fact, every evening they would all go and share the same water hole.

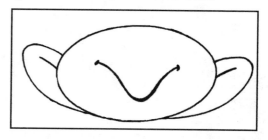

One evening just as they had all gathered around the water hole two large vultures swooped down close to the animals.

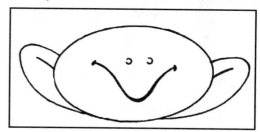

The vultures called for the animals to listen. All was quiet as they told of two hunters that had set up camp at the edge of the savannah. There were two large tents each filled with guns. The animals shuttered at the terrible news.

The animals decided they should find the Sky God and ask for his help. Four monkeys were sent at full speed to find him. They could almost fly through the tree tops and soon had spread out to search the whole forest. Two looked here and here....

...and one looked here

But it was the fourth monkey who found the Sky God here. She quickly told the Sky God about the hunters with all the guns. Sky God smiled and told her to go back to the water hole. There was no need for worry. He would give one of the animals at the water

hole special powers to frighten away the hunters.

The monkey went back to the water hole as she had been directed. She told the animals what the Sky God had said. "But which one of us did the Sky God give the special powers?" they asked one another.

It was getting dark now and the two hunters stuck their heads out of the tents to say goodnight to one another. Just as they did, there was the most hideous, earsplitting sound ever heard in the savannah or the forest. All of the animals shuttered at the sound. It frightened the hunters so that they didn't even bother to pack up their tents. They just ran as fast as they could away from their camp sight and were never seen again. Now to which animal do you think the Sky God gave the special power?

During Reading Activities

Predicting

1. Write the title of the folktale, "How Frog Lost His Tail," on the chalkboard.

2. Now read the following to the children.

   The Sky God took away Frog's tail. But the Sky God did not stop there. He found a way to remind him of how terrible he acted when he had a tail.

3. Encourage the children to predict the story action by asking leading questions, such as:

Why do you think the Sky God took away Frog's tail?

What things might Frog have done to make the Sky God angry?

How do you think the Sky God took away Frog's tail?

4. Copy their suggestions on the chalkboard. The children should now read the story and see if any of their predictions were correct.

After Reading Activities

Pattern writing (p. 8)

This activity sheet will help children with written expression by using a simple writing pattern. You might want to have volunteers share their "stories" with the class. Once illustrated, these might be combined to form an "Frog Wanted..." class book.

Vocabulary expansion (p. 9)

1. Copy the following on a chalkboard or make a thermal transparency.

The (size) (color) Frog (action) to the (sound) water hole.

2. Using the children's suggestions, copy appropriate words in a list under each of the blanks in the sentence. For example, the sentence might look like this after several children have added words.

The (size) (color) Frog (action) to the (sound) water hole.

large	green	hopped	quiet
tiny	brown	tip-toed	noisy
bulky	pink	drove	hushed
puny	yellow	skipped	blaring

3. Now pass out the activity sheet and encourage the children to complete it.

Creative thinking / Story elaboration / Sound story

1. Ask the children what animals they think came to the water hole each evening for a drink. List their responses on the chalkboard.

2. After a while ask for the sounds they think each animal would make. Write these next to the animals' names. Be sure to accept more than one sound per animal! The list might look something like this at the beginning:

Frog—croak

Pig—grunt, squeal, oink

Lion—roar, purr

3. Now organize your "animals" in a concert fashion. Place like animals together and/or children making the same animal sounds together. Practice making their sounds as you direct them, much like a band conductor. When you point to them, they "sound-off"! When you point a second time, they become quiet. You might also control their volume by raising and lowering your other hand. Have fun making a chorus of animal sounds!

4. It is now time for someone to stand next to you and read the story. You will bring in the animal sounds at appropriate times. After practicing this technique a few times, you will want to record your "final take"!

5. Place a copy of the story, along with a tape playback, in your room for children to enjoy.

PATTERN WRITING

*Frog wanted a tail,
so the other animals
would not make fun of him.*

*Humpty Dumpty wanted a net,
so his fall off the wall
would not make scrambled eggs.*

*Snake wanted feet,
so his belly
would not get wet.*

Now You Try It!

_____ wanted _____ ,

*so*_____

would not _____.

Try Another One!

_____ wanted _____ ,

*so*_____

would not _____.

VOCABULARY EXPANSION

Write in words you remember from the story and new ones you think of. Make sure they are the "kind" of words asked for in the sentence. These words will help you when you are ready to write.

The ___(size)___ ___(color)___ Frog ___(action)___ to the ___(sound)___ water hole.

_____	_____	_____	_____
_____	_____	_____	_____
_____	_____	_____	_____
_____	_____	_____	_____
_____	_____	_____	_____
_____	_____	_____	_____

Choose words from these lists to complete this paragraph about the story.

The _____ Frog_____ to the _____
      (color)   (action)   (size)

Sky God. "I want a _____ tail," said Frog. Sky God
                     (size)

looked at Frog for a long time. He then pointed his

_____ finger at the _____ water and
    (size)   (sound)

said, "_____ back to your _____ water hole."
   (action)   (size)

Once there you will hear a _____ sound and see a
                        (sound)

_____ snake. _____ to this_____
   (size)   (Action)   (color)

snake and sit on it. *Then you will have your tail!!!*

THE THREE HARES
FOLKTALE FROM TURKEY

Autumn had arrived. Toysa, Mugla and Hasan, three young rabbits, were playing their favorite game. They were playing "hide the hare," and all their running, hopping and thumping made Father upset.

Father called his sons, "Mugla! Toysa! Hasan! Come here this minute!"

Mugla called, "What do you want, Father?"

Toysa echoed, "What do you want, Father?"

Hasan asked, "Are we too noisy again, Father?"

Father thumped his hind foot and said, "Boys, it's time we had a hare-to-hare talk."

Hasan, Mugla and Toysa quickly ran to their father and skidded to a stop at their hit feet.

"Boys, it's time for you to leave home. You must go out and make homes of your own," said Father. "But beware of Fatsa-the-Fox who likes to eat young rabbits."

And so they left. Each young rabbit looking for the best place to live.

Mugla gathered leaves and grass. With these he quickly built a hut. Mugla looked around his hut and said, "This is a very good hut. I will be very safe here. Even Fatsa-the-Fox cannot get me."

No sooner had Mugla said this than there came a knocking at his door. "This is Fatsa-the-Fox, and you better let me in."

And before Mugla could say a word, Fatsa-the-Fox crashed through his front door. Mugla dashed to Toysa's hut made of sticks. Mugla screamed, "Fatsa-the-Fox is coming. Bolt the door!"

Just then there was a knocking at the door. "This is Fatsa-the-Fox and you better let me in."

Mugla and Toysa just had time to escape as the front door came crashing in. They fled looking for Hasan's hut. When they reached Hasan's hillside they found no hut. Trembling they held one another as Fatsa-the-Fox came bounding over the hill.

"He will eat us. There is no place to hide," they whimpered.

"Mugla! Toysa! Down here!" shouted Hasan.

The two rabbits quickly followed Hasan down his hole to safety. Fatsa-the-Fox stuck his nose into the hole and began digging. Mugla and Toysa screamed, "Your hole is no safer than our huts!"

"Oh yes it is," said Hasan. "Just watch this."

Then Hasan scurried up the hole. He turned around and thumped Fatsa-the-Fox on his nose three times. The fox yelped three times. He pulled his nose out of the hole and never came back again.

Whole-Language Activities for "The Three Hares"

Before Reading Activities

Comparing tales / Story prediction

1. Tell the children that the folktale, "The Three Hares," is from Turkey. It is about three little rabbits and a fox. Their names sound different because they are Turkish names. Say them as you write them on the chalkboard: **Mugla, Toysa, Hasan** and **Fatsa-the-Fox**.

2. Ask the children what they think might happen when three little rabbits and a fox get together. Can they think of other folktales involving three of one animal and one of another? ("Three Billy Goats Gruff," "Three Little Pigs," "Goldilocks and Three Bears," etc.) What happened in these stories? Do they think that something similar will happen in "The Three Hares?" How do they think it will be the same and/or different?

Critical thinking / Story comparisons (p. 13)

This activity sheet will help children think critically by having them compare this story variant with the traditional folktale, "The Three Little Pigs." You might want to encourage a class discussion by using the completed sheets.

Pattern writing (p. 14)

This activity sheet provides a simple writing pattern for students to follow. You will want to obtain a copy of Mercer Mayer's *Just Go to Bed* (Perma-Bound) and present the entire book to the children prior to passing out the sheet.

During Reading Activities

Predictive reading

1. Read aloud the beginning of the story through, "And so they left. Each young rabbit for the best place to live."

2. Now ask the children to guess what the young rabbits will do. Where will they go to live? What will their homes be like? Do they think Fatsa-the-Fox will bother them?

After Reading Activities

Attentive listening/Sound and action story

1. Explain to the children that you will read a shortened version of the story that they have just read. But in this version they will have to listen carefully for different word clues. Each time they hear a word clue they will be expected to create a particular sound and action.

Word Clue	Sound and action
Father	Children will say "Now boys" while shaking index finger.
Mugla	Children will say "Save me!" while holding face in hands.
Toysa	Children will say "Oh no!" while hugging themselves.
Hasan	Children will way "Go away!" while placing hands on hips.
Fatsa-the-Fox	Children will growl while holding up hands to look like claws.

2. Now read the story on the next page as the children attempt to add the sounds.

Once upon a time three young rabbits were making so much noise that their father told them to go make homes of their own.

So Mugla built a hut made of leaves and grass. Toysa built a hut made of sticks. But Hasan did not build a hut. Hasan burrowed deeply in the side of a hill where he made his home.

One day Fatsa-the-Fox knocked on Mugla's door. To get to the rabbit, Fatsa-the-Fox knocked down the hut. Mugla raced to his brother's hut. Toysa and Mugla hid in the hut of sticks. They would not open the door for Fatsa-the-Fox. So he knocked down the second hut. The rabbit brothers fled to find Hasan.

On *Hasan's* hillside, *Mugla* and *Toysa* hugged one another as *Fatsa-the-Fox* approached. *Hasan* led *Mugla* and *Toysa* down the safety of his rabbit hole. *Fatsa-the-Fox* stuck his nose down the hole. *Hasan* said, "Go away, growling *Fatsa-the-Fox*." He then thumped him three times on the nose and saved *Mugla* and *Toysa* from *Fatsa-the-Fox*.

The next day, *Mugla* and *Toysa*, like *Hasan* heeded their *Father's* advice and dug deep holes for their homes.

CRITICAL THINKING / STORY COMPARISONS

How many things can you think of that "The Three Hares" and "The Three Little Pigs" have in common?

The Three Hares

How many little hares?

What was the first hare's hut made of?

What was the second hare's hut made of?

Draw the third hare's home.

The Three Pigs

How many little pigs?

What was the first pig's house made of?

What was the second pig's house made of?

Draw the third pig's home.

The fox tried to get the young rabbits by breaking down their doors.

The wolf tried to get the

_____ by _____

_____ .

The third rabbit got rid of the fox by thumping on his nose.

The third pig got rid of the wolf by _____

_____ .

PATTERN WRITING

Mugla is a cowboy and he rounds up cows. Dad says, "It's time for the cowboy to go to bed."

Fatsa-the-Fox is a space man and he zooms to the moon. Dad says, "It's time for the space man to take a bath."

Jack and Jill are fire fighters and they ride on the truck. Dad says, "It's time to pick up your toys."

Little Boy Blue is a hero on TV and he saves people. Dad says, "You must finish your meal."

Now You Try It!

_____ is a,

_____

Dad says, " _____.

_____ ."

Try Another One!

_____ is a,

_____

Dad says, " _____.

_____ ."

IT COULD ALWAYS BE WORSE

JEWISH FOLKTALE

One day many years ago a man went to a rabbi for advice.

"Oh Rabbi!" he cried. "I do not know what to do. Things are very bad at home. I live in a small house with my wife, her parents and our six children. We are always bumping into one another. There's just not enough room for all of us. We're so poor we can't buy a bigger home. What can I do?"

The rabbi thought for a short time and said, "My son, promise to do as I say and things will get better."

"Oh yes, rabbi. What ever you say."

"Tell me, what animals do you have?"

"I have ducks, pigs and cows."

"Very well, you must bring all of your ducks into your house."

"Rabbi! Ducks?"

"Yes, my son …ducks."

So the man hurried home. He gathered his ducks and guided them into his house.

The next day the man returned to the rabbi. "Rabbi," he cried, "there are ducks everywhere. Ducks in the sink. Ducks on the bed. Ducks under the table. Ducks in the fireplace and ducks on the stove. There are so many ducks there is no room for my family!"

"Ah, now you must bring all of your pigs into your house," said the rabbi.

"Ducks and pigs?" exclaimed the man.

"Yes, my son … ducks and pigs."

So the man hurried home. He gathered his pigs and led them into his house.

The next day the man returned to the rabbi. "Rabbi," he cried, "there are ducks and pigs everywhere. Besides the ducks, there are pigs in the sink. Pigs on the bed. Pigs under the table. Pigs in the fireplace and pigs on the stove. There are so many ducks and pigs there is no room for my family!"

"Ah, now you must bring all of your cows into your house," said the rabbi.

"Ducks, pigs and cows?" exclaimed the man.

"Yes, my son …ducks, pigs and cows."

So the man hurried home and herded the cows into his house.

The next day the man returned to the rabbi. "Rabbi," he cried, "there are ducks, pigs and cows everywhere. Besides the ducks and pigs there are cows in the sink. Cows on the bed. Cows under the table. Cows in the fireplace and cows on the stove. There are so many ducks, pigs and cows there is no room for my family!"

"Ah, now you must take all the animals from your house," said the rabbi.

"Now take the animals out of the house?" exclaimed the man.

"Yes, my son …the animals out of the house."

So the man hurried home and guided the ducks to the pond. He led the pigs to the pen and herded the cows to the barn.

The next day the man hurried to the rabbi. "Rabbi," cried the man, his face beaming, "you have made my life wonderful again. With all of the animals out, the house is so quiet, so roomy and so clean! How can I ever thank you?

The rabbi smiled and told the man to go back to his home and enjoy his splendid life.

Whole-Language Activities for "It Could Always Be Worse"

Before Reading Activities

Story prediction (p. 18)

This activity sheet will help children make predictions about the story. Pass out the activity sheet and ask children to complete it.

After the children complete this sheet, encourage several to share their answers and hold up the drawings. They may then read to find out if their predictions were correct.

During Reading Activities

Interpretive reading / Mood of story

1. Copy the following faces on the chalkboard before beginning the story.

2. Ask the children how they think each of the faces "feel"? Encourage the use of descriptive words, such as happy, sad, angry, frightened, shocked, etc.

3. Now as you read the story, stop at various points (See Suggestion below). Have volunteers go to the chalkboard and point to the appropriate face according to the "feel" of the story. You might want to discuss *why* they choose the faces they do.

   Suggestion: A few good "stopping points" are:
   "I do not know what to do. Things are very bad at home."
   The rabbi thought for a short time.
   "Ducks *and* pigs?" exclaimed the man.
   "You have made my life wonderful again."

Participation reading

1. There is a story segment repeated several times. It is:

   "Ducks in the sink. Ducks on the bed. Ducks under the table. Ducks in the fireplace and ducks on the stove. There are so many ducks there is no room for my family!"

2. Some of the children might recognize the fun of this part and begin to say it with you. Encourage this participation. Repeat it several times so the children feel comfortable with it and then continue reading the story encouraging the children to participate each time you come to the story segment.

After Reading Activities

Story elaboration / Writing pattern (p. 19)

This activity sheet will help children with written expression by using a simple writing pattern. These would make a fun bulletin board entitled, "Animals In Our House!"

Proper story sequence

1. Encourage the students to discuss the story by having each one tell about their favorite parts. Be sure a fairly complete review of the story results. You might want to "fill in" the resulting story omissions.

2. Now have each child draw a scene, of his or her own choosing, from the story. After the drawings are complete ask each student to show and tell about his or her picture. Then have students attempt to arrange themselves and their pictures in the proper story sequence.

   Suggestion: This is best accomplished by having one child at a time go to the front of the group and place herself in the proper order according to the other students already in line.

STORY PREDICTION

Look at the picture.

Why do you think the ducks, pigs and cows are going in the house?

_____

Do you think the family wants them in the house? _____

Where do you think the pigs would go in the house? _____

_____Where would the ducks go? _____

_____What might the cows do?_____

_____

Draw a picture of the house after the animals are all in it.

```



```

STORY ELABORATION / WRITING PATTERN

One day a duck came in my house and laid an egg in the dryer. Mommy did not know it and so we had scrambled laundry.

One day an elephant came in my house and sat on a chair. Daddy did not know it and so he now has peanut shells in his pockets.

Now You Try It!

One day a _____ came in my house,
and _____
_____ did not know it so
_____ .

Try Another One!

One day a _____ came in my house,
and _____
_____ did not know it so
_____ .

THE STRONGEST IN THE FOREST

FOLKTALE FROM VIETNAM

Many years ago, deep in the forest, lived a monkey by the name of Kontum. But that's not what he wanted to be called. This little monkey wanted to be called Kontum-the-Strong. The other monkeys laughed and called him Kontum-the-Dreamer!

"I *am* strong!" shouted Kontum. "I am stronger than Leopard! I am stronger than Tiger. I am the strongest animal in the forest." It wasn't long before Tiger and Leopard heard about Kontum's bragging.

"Is this the home of Kontum?" boomed Tiger.

Kontum looked down from his treetop home and said, "Yes, this is the home of Kontum-the-Strong. What do you want?"

"I want you to come down and we will soon see which of us is the strongest, little one."

"Now Tiger, don't get angry. You only think I'm not strong because of my size. But I know I can beat you in a test of strength."

"What!" laughed Tiger. "That's the silliest thing I have ever heard."

"Well then, just be back here tomorrow morning and we'll have a tug-of-war. Then we'll know who's the strongest in the forest."

Tiger left shaking his head and mumbling to himself.

It wasn't long before the forest shook with Leopard's voice. "I'm looking for Kontum!"

"I'm up here," said Kontum from his treetop house.

"Come down here right now so I can show you who's the strongest in the forest!" boomed Leopard.

"Now Leopard, don't get angry. You only think I'm not strong because of my size. But I know I can beat you in a test of strength."

"Test? What test? What are you talking about?"

"Come back in the morning. We will have a tug-of-war to see who's the strongest in the forest."

"I'll be here. Just make sure *you're* here!" thundered Leopard as he strode off into the forest.

Early the next morning Kontum cut away the longest vine he could find hanging from the tallest tree in the forest. It was so long you could not see the ends. Soon Leopard appeared with a thundering growl.

"Over here, Leopard," said Kontum. "Walk to the end of this vine and when I yell 'tug' the test will begin."

Leopard swaggered into the forest following the vine just as Tiger appeared. "I'm here for the test," he said loudly.

"Good. And I am also ready. Just follow this vine to its end, and when I yell 'tug' the test will begin."

Tiger went off into the forest following the vine in the opposite direction that

Leopard had gone. Kontum waited a few minutes and then loudly yelled, *"TUG!"*

The vine was immediately pulled taunt. Moans and groans could be heard throughout the day as Tiger and Leopard pulled with all their might. Kontum sat in his tree eating a banana and giggling to himself. Finally the vine could take no more and broke. Tiger and Leopard each toppled to the ground completely exhausted.

Kontum wasted no time. He quickly ran to Leopard. "Oh dear," he said finding Leopard flat on the forest floor. "I hope I didn't hurt you."

Leopard looked up weakly and said, "You, Kontum, are indeed the strongest in the forest."

Kontum then ran as fast as he could to the other end of the vine where Tiger was half crouched on the trunk of a large tree. "Are you all right, Tiger?" asked Kontum.

"I am *not* all right! I am exhausted! And you, Kontum, are indeed the strongest in the forest."

Kontum then strutted back to his tree. He climbed up to his tree-branch home and sat, eating a banana. "After all, I have to keep up my strength," he said with a twinkle in his eye.

Whole-Language Activities for "The Strongest in the Forest"

Before Reading Activities

Attentive listening / Fold and cut story

1. You will need a sheet of paper (8 1/2" x 11") and scissors for this story. Fold the sheet of paper in half lengthwise, as shown in the illustration.

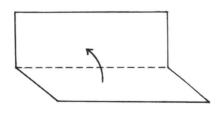

Paper position for story

fold

> **Warning:** Be sure to hold the fold downward and make your cuts exactly as shown in the illustrations: otherwise the finished product will not work.

2. Tell the following story while making the cuts as shown in the illustrations.

> Many years ago a small monkey, by the name of Kontum, lived in the highlands of Vietnam. He was not a happy monkey because his home was *too* crowded. He had so many brothers and sisters that there was no room left for him. Finally the day came when he said "good-bye" to his family and went looking for a new home. He first traveled from the highlands down to the delta.

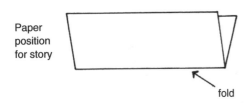

> It was very hot as he walked across the wide flat delta.

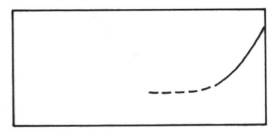

> It was so hot and wet that he decided the delta would not be a good place for his home. Therefore, he stopped a rabbit who was hopping by and asked, "Excuse me, ma'am. But I am looking for a home. Could you please direct me towards a good place to live?"
>
> The rabbit looked surprised and said, "*This* is a very fine place to live. What is wrong with the delta?"
>
> "It's too hot and wet for me," replied Kontum.
>
> "Humph! Well, I suppose you should go to the mountains. There they have forests and jungles you might find more to your liking."
>
> "Yes, that sounds perfect. But which way are the mountains?"
>
> "Follow your nose," said the rabbit as she whirled around and hopped away.
>
> So Kontum "followed his nose." Unfortunately he came to a wide lake and had to go around it.

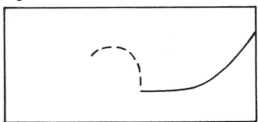

On the other side of the lake, Kontum met a boar getting himself a drink. "Excuse me, sir. But could you tell me which way I would find the mountains?"

The boar said, with water still dripping from his mouth, "Just follow your nose."

And so Kontum continued his trek looking for a good place to in which to build his home. It wasn't long before he came alongside a river. As he sat wondering what to do, he spied a small boat tied to the bank. He immediately hopped into the boat and made his way across the river.

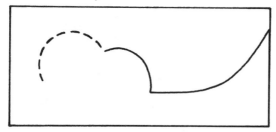

Once on the other side of the river, Kontum saw a goat grazing in a field. "Excuse me, ma'am. Could you tell me how to get to the mountains?"

The goat took a big swallow and said, "Why, you're almost there. Simply follow your nose."

So Kontum quickened his pace and hurried off in the direction of his nose.

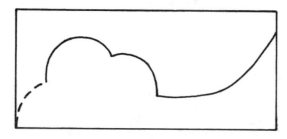

Soon he was climbing the mountains. About half way up one of the highest mountains, Kontum stopped and looking up said, "Oh, this is perfect. I will build my home up there."

Now where do you think Kontum built his home?

(Unfold the paper and show the tree.)

Predictive reading / Sequencing story outline

1. Copy each of the following on a large posterboard strip.

    Monkey thinks he's the strongest in forest.
    Tiger and Leopard become angry.
    A contest is planned to see who is the strongest.
    Monkey cuts a long vine for the contest.
    Tiger and Leopard pull on the vine for a tug-of-war.
    The vine finally breaks.
    Tiger and Leopard think Monkey is the strongest.

2. Tell the children that you have the outline of a folktale they are about to read …but it is all mixed up. You will need their help to try and unravel the order of the story.

3. Read each of the cards you have already prepared, making sure they are not in the correct story sequence. (The outline above is in the correct story sequence.)

4. Using the children's suggestions, place these strips in sequential order on the chalkboard. Use tape or other temporary adhesive so that they may be changed as need be.

During Reading Activities

Story elaboration through dramatization

1. This is a simple story for the children to dramatize as you read. Select volunteers for the three major roles: MONKEY, TIGER and LEOPARD. You will need 3–5 extras to serve as the chorus of MONKEYS who laugh and jeer at Kontum at the beginning of the tale. The only prop you will need is a length of rope.

2. Now have the actors "perform" the tale.

    Suggestion: Prior to acting out the story, you may want to select various episodes to be demonstrated by volunteers. For example:

How would Kontum walk back to his tree after "winning" the contest? or How might Tiger look and act when hearing a monkey was stronger than he was?

After Reading Activities

Writing patterns (p. 25)

This activity sheet provides a simple writing pattern for students to follow.

You may want to create an "I Can" book by compiling all of the children's sheets. Or type the children's responses into a picture book format assigning the children various pages to illustrate. Put a simple cover on this book and place it in your classroom library. This is bound to be one of the children's favorite books!

Story review through mural

1. Use a large sheet of butcher paper or newsprint to create the mural background shown below.

2. Ask the children what "things" from the folktale they think should be part of their mural. You might want to list the suggestions on the chalkboard. After you have a rather complete list, have the children each choose one or two items and draw, color and cut it/them out.

3. The children should now take turns going to the mural, telling about their item(s), how it/they "fit into" the story and taping or pasting it/them onto the mural. When finished, the children may use the mural for retelling of the folktale.

PATTERN WRITING

Think of all the things the monkey, leopard and tiger did in the story. What are other things you *think* they could have done but did not do. List these things below.

walked	jumped
rowed a boat	climbed a tree
sang a song	danced a jig

Now use these words to write the following "I Can" stories.

I can   swim across a wide river   .

Can you   swim across a wide river   ?

I can _____ .

Can you _____ ?

I can _____ .

Can you _____ ?

I can _____ .

Can you _____ ?

THE BALL GAME
CHEROKEE FOLKTALE

Many years ago the Animals and the Birds were going to have a ball game. The ground was made ready. The poles were placed at each end of the field. And the Medicine Man made them a good strong ball to use. Now every important event began with a dance, and so when everything else was ready, it was time for the dance to start.

The Animals were sure they were going to win. They were bigger and stronger than the Birds. And so the Animals danced and danced.

The Birds up in the tree were not so sure they were going to win. Still, they danced in the treetops. Eagle said, "We must play hard. We must play the best we can. And maybe we will win."

The game was about ready to start when Squirrel and Bat came to the Animals. "We are ready to play," said Squirrel.

Bear began to laugh and said, "What do we need with two little animals like yourselves? You can't help us. We don't need any help. We are going to win!"

"But we want to play in the game," said Bat.

"Ho, ho, ho," laughed the Animals. "You can't play ball with us."

Bat and Squirrel were very unhappy. They climbed to the top of the trees where the Birds were dancing. "Please, may we play with you in the ball game?"

Eagle looked at both of them and said, "Neither of you have wings. You are not Birds. You are Animals."

"But the Animals won't let us play with them," cried Bat.

Eagle told the other Birds about Bat and Squirrel. The Birds talked quietly together for a while. And then one of the Birds said, "We could make Bat some wings from the skin stretched over that drum."

Another Bird said, "And we could pull Squirrel's skin between his legs to make wings."

And that is what they did. And soon Bat was flying with his new wings made from drum's skin. And soon Squirrel was learning to fly from tree to tree with his newly stretched wings.

It was now time for the ball game to begin. "Is everyone ready?" called the Medicine Man.

The Animals all shouted, "Yes and we are going to win!"

The Birds nodded yes.

The Medicine Man then tossed the ball into the air. At once the Flying Squirrel swooped down, caught the ball and carried it to the top of the trees. He threw it to one of the Birds, but it was too heavy. The ball fell to the ground.

The Animals cheered as Bear ran after it. But before Bear could get the ball, Bat flew down and grabbed it. Carrying the ball, Bat flew between the poles scoring a point for the Birds. The game continued in this fashion, with the Birds finally winning. The Animals, who were so sure that they were going to win, did not get the ball even once.

After the ball game the Medicine Man gathered the Birds and Animals together. He said, "I hope you learned a lesson today."

"Yes," said Bear not looking up.

"And what is that?" asked the Medicine Man.

"We were too sure we would win the ball game."

"Yes," said the Medicine Man smiling at the birds. "Maybe next time you won't be so sure about winning. And wasn't there another lesson learned?"

The Mountain Lion looked at Bat and Squirrel and said sheepishly, "Bat and Squirrel are small, but they could have helped us to win. I guess you don't have to be big to be good."

"This was a day well spent," said the Medicine Man.

Whole-Language Activities for "The Ball Game"

Before Reading Activities

Story prediction

1. Copy the following on the chalkboard.

   "The Ball Game"

   (A Cherokee Folktale)

   This is a story about a ball game between the Animals and the Birds.

   Who?

   What?

   When?

   Where?

2. Now read the first five paragraphs to the children and have them attempt to answer the four questions on the chalkboard. Copy their answers on the board where appropriate. There may be more than one answer per question.

3. Read the last two paragraphs to the children and ask for volunteers to suggest what takes place in the story. You might want to list a variety of guesses on the board.

4. Now read the story and see if any of your predictions are correct.

Vocabulary prediction (p. 31)

This activity sheet will direct your children to think about the possible vocabulary they will encounter in the folktale. This is accomplished through an ABC format.

After they complete this sheet, read the story to find out how many of their words were included. Their finished papers might be assembled on a bulletin board entitled "The ABCs of 'A Ball Game.'"

During Reading Activities

Story prediction (p. 32)

1. The children will each need a copy of this activity sheet to use as you read the folktale.

2. You will stop reading, at various times, (indicated below) and have the children illustrate a "photo" of what they think will happen next in the story.

Prediction Points (stop reading & draw)

…And maybe we will win. (page 26, paragraph 3)

… "But we want to play in the game," said Bat. (page 26, paragraph 6)

… "Please, may we play with you in the ball game?" (page 26, paragraph 8)

…The Medicine Man then tossed the ball into the air. (page 26, Paragraph 17)

…The Animals cheered as Bear ran after it. (page 26, paragraph 18)

…He said, "I hoped you learned a lesson today." (page 27, paragraph 1)

After Reading Activities

Attentive listening / Sound story

1. Explain to the children that you will read a shortened version of the story that they have just read. But in this version they will have to listen carefully for different word clues.

2. Each time they hear a word clue they will be expected to create a particular sound. Assign groups of children to each of the following word clues. Only these children are to make the appropriate sound for their clue word. The first two word clues, though, are made by the entire class.

Word Clue	Sound
Animals	Chatter chatter (whole class)
Birds	Tweet tweet (whole class)
Medicine Man	Play ball (group 1)
Bear	Growl growl (group 2)
Squirrel	Crack crack (group 3)
Bat	Flap flap (group 4)
Eagle	Screech screech (group 5)

3. Now read the story slowly as the children add the sounds.

Many years ago the **Animals** wanted to play a ball game. They went to the **Medicine Man** and asked his advice. He suggested that they ask the **Birds** to play with them. So it was decided …the **Birds** and the **Animals** would play a game of ball and the **Medicine Man** would be in charge.

Squirrel and **Bat** wanted to be on the **Animals'** team but **Bear** just laughed and said they were too small. So **Squirrel** and **Bat** went to the **Birds** and asked to be on their team. **Eagle** asked the **Birds** and they agreed to let **Squirrel** and **Bat** play on their team.

The **Medicine Man** threw the ball in the air, and the game began. Flying **Squirrel** swooped down and caught the ball. The **Animals** jumped high but could not get it from **Squirrel**. The **Birds** all cheered. But then **Squirrel** dropped the ball and all the **Animals** cheered. Before **Bear** could get the ball, **Bat** flew down and grabbed it. He carried it above the **Animals'** heads and made the first point. The game continued in this way, with the **Birds** winning.

After the game the **Medicine Man** called all the **Birds** and **Animals** together.

He asked what lesson they had learned. **Bear** said, "We were too sure we would win the game."

"Yes," agreed the **Medicine Man**. "And what other lesson?"

The **Mountain Lion** looked at **Bat** and **Squirrel** and said, "You don't have to be big to win."

"Very good," said the **Medicine Man**. The **Animals** and **Birds** all cheered.

Story elaboration / Creative dramatics

1. Line the children up as though they were sitting in a grandstand watching a ball game. (Three rows will work nicely, with the first row sitting on the floor, the second on chairs and the third standing.)

2. Tell the children that you will read a short account of the ball game. They are to pretend they are on the Bird's side and so should show how happy they are when something good happens to the Birds and, of course, how sad they are when the Birds do not do so well. All of their expression, though, is to be through pantomime. No sound is to be made. They must show their emotions through facial expressions and body gestures.

Suggestion: It is a good idea to practice looking sad and happy before beginning the story. Have volunteers show how they would look/act.

3. Now slowly read the following brief account of the ball game as you encourage the children to react.

The Medicine Man tossed the ball into the air. At once the Flying Squirrel swooped down, caught the ball and carried it to the top of the trees. He threw it to one of the Birds but it was too heavy for the bird to catch. The ball fell to the ground. Bear grabbed it and ran down the field. The Animals cleared a path so Bear could run the ball right between the poles.

As Bear neared the poles he tripped on a stick on the playing field and fell head-over-heels. The ball flew out of his hands and was caught by Bat. Bat then quickly passed it to Eagle who flew the ball back down the field and between the poles. The Birds had scored their first point.

The Animals then had the ball. Down the field ran Mountain Lion with the ball in his mouth. The Birds scattered as he sprinted past them. He passed the ball to Goat who took the ball through the poles. The score was now one to one.

It was nearing the end of the game and the Birds had the ball. Eagle passed it over the heads of the Animals to Pelican who caught it in his large mouth. With the ball safe in his mouth he flew down to the poles. With only three seconds to spare, Pelican tossed the ball to the ground. It rolled towards the poles as Elephant tried to jump on it. He missed and the ball kept rolling. Giraffe and Zebra collided into one another as they ran after the ball. As the Birds and Animals watched, the ball rolled through the poles. The Birds had won the game.

VOCABULARY PREDICTION

The Animals and the Birds are going to play a
ball game. What words do you think you
might find in this story? Make an "ABC Ball
Game" list of words below. A few have
already been filled in. Now you try the others.

A - _____

B - _____Bear, Ball, Beat_____

C - _____Cheer, Camel, Call_____

D - _____

E - _____

F - _____

G - _____Goal, Goat, Go_____

H - _____

I - _____

J - _____

K - _____

L - _____

M- _____

N - _____

O - _____Owl, Ouch, Out_____

P - _____

Q - _____

R - _____

S - _____

T - _____

U - _____

V - _____

W- _____

X - _____

Y - _____

Z - _____

STORY PREDICTION

THE BALL GAME

(1)

(2)

(3)

(4)

(5)

(6)

THE THREE WISHES

RUSSIAN FOLKTALE

One rainy spring day many years ago a little old man's cart became stuck in the mud. "Help me!" he cried. But the people walked by him as if he wasn't there. "Please, help me!" he continued to cry. But no one stopped. He became very tired and sat down to think.

"Pardon me," said Ivan, a young peasant boy. "Do you need help with your cart?"

"Oh, yes. It is stuck and I can't pull it out. I asked for help but no one would stop," said the little old man.

"Let me try," said Ivan. So with Ivan pulling and the old man pushing, the cart was soon free from the mud.

"Here, let me pay you," said the little old man putting his hand in his pocket.

"There is no need for payment," smiled Ivan. "I'm glad to have helped."

The little old man looked closely at the young peasant. He smiled a wee smile and said, "I will give you something better than the Tsar's gold. I will give you three wishes. Now what do you wish for?"

Ivan thought for a long time and said, "First, I wish for a bow and arrow that will always hit its mark. Second, I wish for a balalaika that will make everyone dance when it is played. Third, I wish that whenever I ask anyone for something, I will get it right away."

"You have your three wishes," said the little old man.

In a moment the little old man was gone, and Ivan had a beautiful balalaika in his arms. And on the grass beside him, there was a bow and arrow.

Ivan walked down the road as happy as the Tsar. He soon met a man who was looking up into a tall tree.

"Good day to you," said Ivan. "What are you looking at up in the tree?"

"See that beautiful bird up in the tree?" said the man. "I would give anything if I could have that beautiful bird."

"And you shall have it," said Ivan. He took his bow and arrow and nicked the bird's wing. It fell to the ground. The man picked up the bird and hurried down the road without even saying "thank you." This made Ivan very angry. And so he picked up his balalaika and began to play. And the man began to dance. Faster and faster Ivan played on the balalaika. And faster and faster the man danced.

"Stop, stop!" cried the man. "Stop playing that balalaika so I can stop dancing."

"What will you give me?" asked Ivan.

"One hundred rubles," cried the man.

Ivan stopped playing the balalaika. The man was so tired that he fell down on the ground. But he put his hand in his pocket and gave Ivan the hundred rubles.

Ivan took the money and went on down the road humming to himself.

Pretty soon the man got up and went to the nearest town. He went to the Judge of the town and said, "A man robbed me of a hundred rubles." And he described for the Judge just how Ivan looked.

Soon Ivan was brought in to the Judge. They found the hundred rubles in his pocket, and so the Judge said that Ivan must be punished.

Ivan said, "Before I am punished, please let me play my balalaika."

The man cried, "No, no, no!"

But then Ivan's third wish came true, and the Judge said, "You may play on your balalaika."

Ivan began to play on his balalaika, and the Judge and the man began to dance. Ivan played faster and faster. And the Judge and the man danced faster and faster.

The Judge cried out, "Enough! I can't dance any more!"

"Then have the man tell the truth," cried Ivan.

"Tell the truth," ordered the Judge.

"I will tell the truth," said the man, "only have him stop playing."

And so Ivan stopped playing on his balalaika. And when the man had gotten his breath he told the true story and how he had lied.

The Judge then said that the man must be punished. And he told Ivan to leave. "Go quickly," said the Judge, "and never play your balalaika in our town again."

Ivan went on his way. He lived a long and happy life, and he died a very rich man.

Whole-Language Activities for "The Three Wishes"

Before Reading Activities

Brainstorming story possibilities (p. 36)

This activity sheet is designed to help students work through a simple discussion of the possible elements of the story they are to read. Have the children complete the sheet prior to the discussion.

Now encourage them to share and compare their ideas during the brainstorming session.

During Reading Activities

Story interpretation / Creative dramatics

This folktale is filled with action, making it quite suitable for creative dramatics. There are many times throughout the story you will want to stop reading and "act out" the scene just read. Simply choose volunteers for the small cast and have them recreate the short scene just finished.

After the scene has been acted out, ask for ways in which to improve the scene. After several suggestions, have the actors repeat the scene.

Here are a few scenes particularly suitable for acting out.

Scene	Characters
Ivan helping man with cart.	Ivan/old man
Ivan receiving three wishes from the old man.	Ivan/old man
Ivan getting bird for man.	Ivan/man
Ivan playing balalaika so man could not stop dancing.	Ivan/man
Ivan brought to the Judge.	Ivan/man/Judge
Ivan playing balalaika so man & Judge dance.	Ivan/man/Judge

After Reading Activities

Pattern writing (p. 37)

This activity sheet will help improve the children's writing skills through pattern writing.

Attach the children's finished papers to a bulletin board with the following heading.

Look! See our papers.
They are really super.

Summarizing through art

1. Begin this activity by asking the children what "things" they remember from the story. Copy some of their suggestions on the chalkboard.

2. After several "things" are on the board, explain that they are to draw as many items from the story as they can remember.

3. Each child should hold up their art and tell the "things" they drew. Be sure to continue listing the items not previously on the board.

4. After the list is complete, ask for volunteers to come to the board. Each volunteer is to choose two items listed on the chalkboard and tell what connection they had in the story. For example, suppose the two items chosen were an arrow and a bird. The child might say, "The boy shot the bird with the arrow."

BRAINSTORMING STORY POSSIBILITIES

THE THREE WISHES

This story takes place a very long time ago
in Russia. It is springtime and a young
peasant boy, Ivan, is given three wishes.
Now answer the following questions.

Who do you think gave Ivan his three wishes?

_____

Why was Ivan given the three wishes?

_____

Make drawings showing each of Ivan's wishes.

Ivan is taken to a Judge. Do you think his wishes will help him?

_____   How might they?_____

_____

This is how Ivan looks at the end of the story.

PATTERN WRITING

Look! See the old man's cart.
It is stuck in the mud.

Look! See the arrow.
It is flying through the air.

Look! See the balalaika.
It is making everyone dance

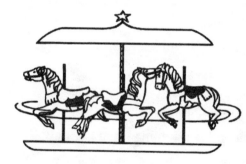

Look! See the merry-go-round.
It is going very fast.

Now You Try It!

Look! See the_____ .

It is_____ .

Look! See the_____ .

It is_____ .

Look! See the_____ .

It is_____ .

THE THREE BILLY GOATS GRUFF

A FOLKTALE FROM NORWAY

Characters: Narrator, First Billy Goat, Second Billy Goat, Third Billy Goat, Troll.

Narrator: Once upon a time three Billy Goats lived on a hill. They had lived on the hill a long time. They liked the sweet grass that grew there. The three Billy goats ate the grass every day. But the grass did not last very long.

First Billy Goat: The grass on this hill grows thin.

Second Billy Goat: Yes, we have eaten much grass. It is almost gone.

First Billy Goat: What shall we do? I am hungry.

Second Billy Goat: We cannot stay here. There is not enough grass to feed us.

Third Billy Goat: We must go down the hill into the valley. Sweet, thick grass grows there. Surely there will be enough grass to feed us for a long time.

Narrator: The three Billy Goats went down the hill. At the bottom of the hill was a bridge. The first Billy Goat stepped onto the bridge. His feet made a noise like trip trip trip.

Troll: Who's that tripping on my bridge?

First Billy Goat: It is only I—the smallest Billy Goat Gruff. I am going to the valley to eat the sweet grass.

Troll: You are on my bridge! I am coming to gobble you up!

First Billy Goat: Oh, please don't gobble me up.

Troll: Why?

First Billy Goat: I am too little. Wait a bit longer. My brother is coming. He is much larger than I am.

Troll: Very well. I will wait.

Narrator: The Second Billy Goat then stepped onto the bridge. His feet made a noise like tramp, tramp, tramp.

Troll: Who's that tramping on my bridge?

Second Billy Goat: It is I—the smallest Billy Goat Gruff's older brother. I am going to the valley to eat the sweet grass there.

Troll: Yes, your brother said you would come. You are on my bridge. I am coming to gobble you up.

Second Billy Goat: Oh, please don't gobble me up.

Troll: Why?

Second Billy Goat: I am too little. Wait a bit longer. My brother is coming. He is much larger than I am.

Troll: Very well. I will wait.

Narrator: The Third Billy Goat stepped onto the bridge. His feet made a noise like tromp, tromp, tromp.

Troll: Who's that tromping on my bridge?

Third Billy Goat: It is I—the largest Billy Goat Gruff.

Troll: Yes, your brother said you would come. You are on my bridge. I am coming to gobble you up.

Third Billy Goat: Yes, come and gobble me up if you can! I will wait!

Troll: Here I come!

Narrator: The hungry troll climbed onto the bridge. The Third Billy Goat lowered his head. The troll stepped toward the Billy Goat. The Billy Goat charged the troll. The Billy Goat knocked the troll off of the bridge. And the troll was never seen again.

Whole-Language Activities for "The Three Billy Goats Gruff"

Before Reading Activities

Vocabulary prediction (p. 42)

1. This activity sheet will help children make predictions about the story and about the language used in the story; it will also help them to use associative thinking by using two new words in one sentence.

2. After the children have completed the activities, encourage several to share their answers.

3. The children should now read the story to find out if their predictions were correct.

Description (p. 43)

Have children examine the drawing of the troll and then choose words that they think best describe it. This will be a special help to children who don't know what a troll is.

As they read the story, the children can confirm or deny the validity of their descriptive choices.

In order for children to develop flexible thinking, have them use words from the list to use as the basis for the construction of similes. This activity will help the children stretch their perceptions, thinking and language patterns.

Oral inflection (p. 44)

Since this story is written in play format, the children may want to practice reading aloud for different vocal/emotional meanings.

1. Pass out the activity sheet and then, either as a group or individually, have the children read each sentence slowly, making sure to emphasize each word in italics.

2. After reading each sentence, ask the children what each sentence means, and also why each sentence means something different.

During Reading Activities

Interpretive reading / Vocal emphasis and collaborative reading

1. Ask each student who is to read a part to underline one word in each line that he/she reads; the underlined word will be the word that the student emphasizes.

2. Now have the students read the play emphasizing the appropriate words they underlined. This might be done in one of the following ways:

    a. One way to share this story is to assign parts for some of the children to read aloud to the entire class.

    b. Another idea might be for small groups of students to read each part—a group reads the troll, a group reads the First Billy Goat, etc.

    c. Yet another idea might be for the class to break into groups of five so that each group reads the play and each student has a part.

After Reading Activities

Vocabulary extension (p. 45)

1. Copy the following on the chalkboard.

    A -
    B -
    C -
    D -
    E -

2. Now ask the children to think back to the story and think of words, phrases or sentences in which one of the words begin with the letters on the board. It is important to note that these words need not have been used in the story, but could be words that somehow relate to the story. For example:

A - across the bridge

B - the troll was a bully

C - I am coming to gobble you up.

D - down the hill

E - Troll's stomach was empty.

3. Now pass out the activity sheet and encourage the children to complete it.

Writing with exaggeration (p. 46)

1. Encourage the children to discuss the fact that in the story the troll and the three goats were very hungry. Have they ever been very hungry? How did it make them feel?

2. Now pass out the activity sheet and have the children complete it. You will probably want to work the children through it as a class activity.

VOCABULARY PREDICTION

The story of "The Three Billy Goats Gruff" is about three goats that want to cross a bridge to eat sweet grass. Which of the following words do you think will be in the story?

bridge	water
rabbit	troll
goat	grass
tramp	hill
sneeze	cry
brother	little
horn	gobble
hungry	valley
noise	knock

Use each pair of words in a sentence:

1. brother and hungry
2. gobble and grass
3. noise and bridge
4. valley and hill
5. gobble and goat

Read the story "The Three Billy Goats Gruff," then go back and circle the words from the list that were in the story.

DESCRIPTION

Choose words from below that you think best describe this troll.

happy	angry
cranky	beautiful
sad	dirty
hungry	loud
silly	short
funny	big
mean	sweet
bright	huge
nutty	ugly
lonely	rotten
loving	unloved
afraid	scary

Writing Pattern: Similes

Complete the following: (in the first blank goes a word from the list above)

The troll was a_____ as a _____ .

Example:
The troll was as <u>lonely</u> as a <u>baby bird left alone in his nest</u>.
The troll was as <u>scary</u> as <u>my basement at night!</u>

ORAL INFLECTION

Read each sentence aloud and emphasize the *italicized* word.
Notice how the meaning of each sentence changes.

1. ***Who*** is that tramping on my bridge?

2. Who is ***that*** tramping on my bridge?

3. Who is that ***tramping*** on my bridge?

4. Who is that tramping ***on*** my bridge?

5. Who is that tramping on ***my*** bridge?

6. Who is that tramping on my ***bridge***?

7. Oh, ***please*** don't gobble me up.

8. Oh, please ***don***'t gobble me up.

9. Oh, please don't ***gobble*** me up.

10. Oh, please don't gobble ***me*** up.

VOCABULARY EXTENSION / STORY REVIEW

THE THREE BILLY GOATS GRUFF

Write in words, phrases or sentences you remember from the story, but at least one word *must* begin with that alphabet letter.

These words do not have to be in the story. They may be words the story made you think about.

A - _____

B - _____

C - _____

D - _____

E - _____

F - _____

G - _____

H - _____

I - _____

J - _____

K - _____

L - _____

M - _____

N - _____

O - _____

P - _____

Q - _____

R - _____

S - _____

T - _____

U - _____

V - _____

W- _____

X - _____

Y - _____

Z - _____

WRITING WITH EXAGGERATION

THE THREE BILLY GOATS GRUFF

In the story of "The Three Billy Goats Gruff," the three goats and the troll were very hungry. The three goats wanted to eat sweet grass and the troll wanted to eat the goats. Using your imagination, how many different ways can you complete the following sentences?

1. The three goats were so hungry that they could have eaten_____

    _____.

2. The troll was so hungry that he could have eaten _____

    _____.

Here are some examples:

The three goats were so hungry that they could have eaten <u>all the grass in the entire valley</u>.

The three goats were so hungry that they could have eaten <u>a whole barn-full of hay</u>.

The three goats were so hungry that they could have eaten <u>the troll's bridge</u>.

The troll was so hungry that he could have eaten <u>all three billy goats</u>.

The troll was so hungry that he could have eaten <u>an elephant if one had been there</u>.

The troll was so hungry that he could have eaten <u>the moon because it looked like green cheese</u>.

SNAKE LOSES HIS DINNER

A FOLKTALE FROM MEXICO

Characters: Narrator, Snake, Mouse, Coyote.

Narrator: It was a very hot day in the desert. It was so hot that even Snake was looking for a shady place to rest. he crawled under a rock and fell asleep. When he woke up he discovered that the rock had shifted. Snake was trapped!

Snake: Help! Help! somebody help me. Let me out of here. I'm trapped!

Narrator: At that moment, Mouse was scurrying by. She stopped when she heard Snake's cry for help.

Mouse: Hello. Hello, is there someone there?

Snake: Please, help me. I am trapped beneath this rock and I am so weak and hot that I cannot move it.

Mouse: I will try. Be patient and I will try and move the rock.

Snake: Please hurry.

Narrator: Mouse began pushing and shoving with all her tiny might. She strained against the rock. Finally, it began to move. Mouse budged the rock just enough so that Snake could escape.

Snake: Thank you for freeing me, little mouse.

Mouse: You're welcome. And now I must be on my way.

Snake: Not so fast! I am hungry. I think I will have you for my dinner!

Mouse: But you can't. I saved you. You can't eat me!

Snake: Oh, yes I can.

Narrator: At that moment, Coyote happened to be passing by. He stopped when he heard Mouse cry for help.

Mouse: Help! Help! Someone please help me!

Coyote: What is the trouble, Mouse?

Mouse: Snake is going to eat me. And I just saved his life! It is not fair.

Coyote: You saved his life? How did you save his life, Mouse?

Mouse: I pushed away the rock that had trapped him.

Coyote: I see. Now, let me be sure I understand. Mouse was trapped under a rock, and Snake saved her.

Mouse: No, no. That is not right at all.

Coyote: Well then, who was trapped beneath the rock? I do not understand.

Snake: I was the one who was trapped.

Coyote: You were trapped?

Snake: Yes, I was trapped.

Coyote: I am afraid that I still do not understand. Perhaps you could show me what happened. Then I will not be confused.

Snake: Oh, very well. But let us hurry. I am hungry.

Narrator: With that, Snake crawled back under the rock. Mouse pushed the rock on top of Snake.

Coyote: Oh, I see. Snake was trapped.

Mouse: Yes.

Snake: Yes, I was trapped.

Coyote: Yes, now I understand. Snake was trapped.

Snake: I am glad that you understand. Now let me out.

Coyote: What was that you said?

Snake: I said, let me out!

Coyote: I think that perhaps Mouse should decide whether to move the rock again.

Snake: Let me out!

Coyote: Good-bye, snake. Good-bye, Mouse.

Mouse: Good-bye, Coyote. Thank you for your help.

Snake: Let me out! Somebody help me!

Mouse: Snake, can you hear me?

Snake: Yes, I can hear you.

Mouse: Good. I just wanted to say one thing to you.

Snake: What?

Mouse: Good-bye.

Narrator: And Mouse went on her way. As for snake, well, he is probably still under that rock, calling for help.

Whole-Language Activities for "Snake Loses His Dinner"

Before Reading Activities

Facts and understanding (p. 51)

1. Find pictures of a mouse, a snake and a coyote for the children to examine.

2. Then have them complete the activity sheet by thinking of words that describe each animal.

3. Next, have the children make a list of places where each animal might live.

4. The children should then make a list of things that the animals cannot do. Good questions might be: Why can't the animals do the things on our list? In what places might these animals live together? How are these animals alike?

Paragraph building (p. 52)

This activity sheet is designed to help children examine a problem from different points of view, make a decision based upon their examinations and then write about the decision in a paragraph.

1. The children should make a list of words that they associate with the word "snake."

2. Then children should group their words into at least two categories—this promotes flexible thinking and helps the children establish new patterns of conceptual understanding.

3. Next have the children list possible positive and negative effects of freeing the trapped snake.

4. Based on the work the children have done thus far, they should now decide whether to free the snake.

5. Have children should give one reason why they would or would not free the snake.

6. When finished, have the class share their answers and then group together those answers that seem to have something in common.

7. After grouping the answers, have the class put them together in paragraphs with this as the topic sentence: I would (would not) free the trapped snake because...

Story prediction (p. 53)

1. Copy the following on the chalkboard.

   Monday

   Tuesday

   Wednesday

   Thursday

   Friday

   Saturday   I'm back under the rock. I'm calling for help but nobody will help me.

2. Ask the children if they know what a diary is. Explain that it is something in which a person writes every day. The person writes briefly about what happened during that day.

3. Read the following to the children: "and Mouse went on her way. As for Snake, well, he is probably still under that rock, calling for help."

4. Explain that they should pretend they are the snake. Ask them to think about what might have happened to the snake on

each day, and how he ended up under the rock, calling for help on Saturday.

5. Now pass out the activity sheet and encourage the children to complete it.

During Reading Activities

Group reading

One technique for helping children to enjoy this story is to divide the class into three groups: mouse group, snake group, coyote group (one child serves as narrator).

Each group draws or cuts out of paper a sign or mask to be worn during reading.

As each group reads the story, they might also want to pay attention to the kind of voice they use as the characters: the mouse voice might be high pitched, the snake voice soft and full of hisses and the coyote voice calm but strong.

After Reading Activities

Story sequence (p. 54)

In order to insure critical comprehension of the story, use the story sequence activity sheet.

1. Divide children into pairs or small groups and distribute the sequence strips. The children should then arrange the strips in the order of the story.

2. Children may reread the story to verify their choices.

Pattern writing (p. 55)

This activity sheet will help children with written expression by using a simple writing pattern.

1. Pass out the activity sheet and help the children get started by reading through the directions with them. You might want to do a class pattern on the chalkboard prior to having the children work individually on the sheet.

2. Now have volunteers share their "stories" with the class. Once illustrated, these might be combined to form a "But Then..." class book.

SNAKE LOSES HIS DINNER

List words that describe:

Mouse	Snake	Coyote

List places where each animal might live:

Mouse	Snake	Coyote

List words that describe what each animal *cannot* do:

Mouse	Snake	Coyote

In what places might these animals live together?

_____

How are these animals alike?

_____

SNAKE LOSES HIS DINNER

Read the following:

It was a very hot day in the desert. It was so hot that even
Snake was looking for a shady place to rest. He crawled
under a rock and fell asleep. When he woke up he discovered
that the rock had shifted. Snake was trapped!

 Snake then called for help, "Help! Help! Somebody help
me. Let me out of here. I'm trapped!"

Answer the following:

Make a list of all the words you think of when you hear the word snake.

Group your words into at least two categories.

Based on your list of words, would you let Snake out of his trap?

Now, give a reason why you would, or why you would not let Snake out of
his trap.
I would not let Snake out of his trap because _____
_____.

I would not let Snake out of his trap because _____
_____.

Look at all the reasons give. How many are alike? How many are not alike?

Which answers seem to go together?

STORY PREDICTION

SNAKE'S PICTURE DIARY

Monday

Tuesday

Wednesday

Thursday

Friday

Saturday

SNAKE LOSES HIS DINNER

Place the following events in the order in which they appeared in the story.

Mouse asks Coyote for help.

Snake crawls under the rock to show Coyote what happened.

Mouse pushes the rock to free Snake, who is trapped.

Mouse scurries through the desert and hears Snake's voice.

Mouse says good-bye to Snake.

Coyote asks Mouse to explain what happened.

Coyote doesn't understand why Snake and Mouse are arguing.

Snake tries to eat Mouse.

Coyote says good-bye to Mouse.

PATTERN WRITING

Mouse helped snake get out of the hole.
          BUT THEN
Snake tried to eat Mouse.
          SO
Coyote tricked Snake back into the hole.

                    Little Boy Blue helped the sheep go to the barn.
                              BUT THEN
                    The sheep tried to go back to the meadow.
                              SO
                    Little boy blue locked the barn door.

Now you try it!

_____helped_____ to_____.

                    BUT THEN

_____ tried to_____.

                    SO

_____.

Try another one!!!

_____helped_____ to_____.

                    BUT THEN

_____ tried to_____.

                    SO

_____.

STORY INTEGRATION WHOLE-LANGUAGE ACTIVITIES

Pattern writing (p. 58)

1. Copy the following on the chalkboard:

Mugla	Rabbi	Kontum
Squirrel	Ivan	Frog
Troll	Snake	

2. Tell the children that these are characters from the folktales. Ask for the names of other characters they remember. Use their suggestions to extend the list on the board.

3. Now pass out the activity sheet and encourage the children to complete it.

Critical thinking / Character analysis (p. 59)

Prior to passing out the activity sheet you may want to encourage the children to discuss as many of the characters as they can remember from the various folktales.

Creative thinking / Oral communication

1. Each child is to think of one of their favorite characters in the folktales. Now have them think of something that happened to their character.

2. Have volunteers come to the front of the classroom and act out the scene. Those in the audience may guess the character and folktale.

Story elaboration / Pattern writing (p. 60)

1. Ask the children to name a character from one of the stories. Now ask them to suppose the character was going to go shopping. What do they think he might buy? Maybe the Troll would buy a net with which to catch the Billy Goats.

2. Pass out the activity sheet and encourage the children to complete it.

Critical thinking

1. Ask the students to remember the story about "How Frog Lost His Tail." Can anyone remember the story? Did Frog have a tail at the beginning of the story? How did he get one? How did he lose it?

2. Now ask them to think of a character from another of the folktales. Imagine that this character lost something. Tell how he lost it. For example:

   Troll used to have large horns growing out of his head.

   But the Third Billy Goat Gruff knocked them off when he pushed him off the bridge.

3. Divide the children into small groups and have each group think of a character that has lost something. They must also decide how it was lost.

4. Each group will now take turns saying the character and the "thing" lost. The

rest of the class must guess how the character lost it. After several guesses, have the group tell their reason.

Creative thinking / Oral communication

1. You will need a grocery sack filled with various items, such as a balloon, a pencil, a paper clip, a ball, a spoon, a piece of string, a toy car, etc.

2. Ask volunteers to come to the front of the classroom, pull out an object from the sack and tell to which folktale character they think it belongs. Why? For example:

   A wad of cotton would belong to the poor man in "It Could Always Be Worse" because he could stuff it into his ears. That way he wouldn't hear all of the noise in his house filled with people and animals.

Critical thinking / Pattern writing *(p. 61)*

This activity sheet will help improve the children's writing skills through pattern writing.

Attach the children's finished papers to a bulletin board with the following heading.

"Ooops, We Were Wrong!"

Important: It will be necessary to help the children work through the writing pattern the first time. You might want to do the first pattern as a group story. You will note that the children are expected to find a partner with which to work through most of the sheet. You may want to monitor this activity!

Fatsa-the-Fox wanted a hare.
So he crashed down the hare's home.
But the hare ran away.

Troll wanted a Billy Goat.
So he hid under the bridge.
But the Billy Goat knocked
him off the bridge.

Now you try! But you must use the characters from the stories.
Look on the chalkboard for ideas.

_____wanted_____.

So he_____.

But the _____.

Now see how silly you can make one. For example:

The Frog wanted to fly.
So he glued feathers on his feet.
But the feathers tickled him so that he
couldn't stop laughing.

_____wanted_____.

So he_____.

But the _____.

CRITICAL THINKING / CHARACTER ANALYSIS

You are having a birthday party.

You may invite three of the characters from the stories.

Draw the pictures of whom you are inviting.

Write their names under the pictures.

Now tell why you are inviting them.

The first one is an example.

_____Ivan_____
Character

Because he can grant wishes.

He could give me anything I

wanted.

_____
Character

_____
Character

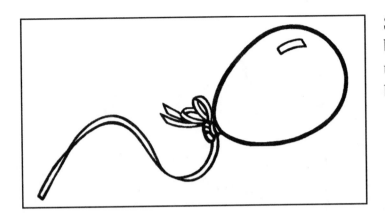

Snake would buy a balloon. He could slip it under the rock and when he blew the rock would move.

Now You Try!

_____would

buy a_____.

Because_____

_____

_____.

_____would

buy a_____.

Because_____

_____

_____.

There is Ivan.

He is playing in the ball game.

Oh dear, I was wrong. That is Squirrel!

Can you do this?

Fill in the name of someone from a story. Now have him do something that someone else from a different story would do. Then tell who <u>that</u> person is.

Try this one with your class!

There is_____,

He is_____.

Oh dear, I was wrong. That is_____.

You try one!

There is_____,

He is_____.

Oh dear, I was wrong. That is_____.

Now find a partner and do the rest.

There is_____,

He is_____.

Oh dear, I was wrong. That is_____.

There is_____,

He is_____.

Oh dear, I was wrong. That is_____.

BIBLIOGRAPHY OF MULTICULTURAL CHILDREN'S BOOKS

Aardema, Verna. *Bringing the Rain to Kapiti Plain: A Nandi Tale.* Dial, 1981.

———. *What's So Funny,* Ketu? Dial, 1982.

———. *Who's in Rabbit's House?* Dial, 1977.

———. *Why Mosquitoes Buzz in People's Ears.* Dial, 1975.

———. *The Riddle of the Drum.* Four Winds, 1979.

Adoff, Arnold. *All the Colors of the Race.* Lothrop, Lee & Shepard, 1982.

———. *Black is Brown.* Harper & Row, 1973.

Agard, John. *The Calypso Alphabet.* Holt, 1989.

Aliki, *Corn is Maize.* Crowell, 1976.

Asch, Frank and Vladimir Vagin. *Here Comes the Cat!* Scholastic, 1989.

Baker, Betty. *Rat Is Dead and Ant Is Sad.* Harper & Row, 1981.

Baker, Olaf. *Where the Buffaloes Begin.* Warne, 1981.

Barett, Joyce Durham. *Willie's Not the Hugging Kind.* Harper & Row, 1989.

Baylor, Byrd. *The Desert Is Theirs.* Scribner's Sons, 1975.

———. *Hawk, I'm Your Brother.* Scribner, 1976.

———. *When Clay Sings.* Scribner's Sons, 1972.

———. *Moonsong.* Scribner's Sons, 1982.

———. *The Other Way to Listen.* Scribner's Sons, 1978.

Behrens, June. *Fiesta!* Children's Press, 1978.

Belpre, Pura. *The Rainbow-Colored Horse.* Warne, 1978.

Bierhorst, John. *A Cry From the Earth.* Four Winds, 1979.

Brown, Marcia *Shadow.* Scribner, 1983.

Brown, Tricia. *Hello Amigos.* Holt, Rinehart & Winston, 1986.

Bryan, Ashley. *Beat the Story-Drum, Pum-Pum.* Atheneum, 1980.

———. *The Dancing Granny.* Macmillan, 1977.

———. *Turtle Knows Your Name.* Atheneum, 1989.

Bulla, Clyde. *Conquista.* Crowell, 1978.

Caines, Jeanette. *Abby.* Harper & Row, 1973.

Carew, Jan. *The Third Gift.* Little, Brown, 1974.

Cleaver, Elizabeth. *The Enchanted Caribou.* Atheneum, 1985.

Clifton, Lucille. *Everett Anderson's Goodbye.* Holt, Reinhart & Winston, 1983.

Climo, Shirley. *The Egyptian Cinderella.* Crowell, 1989.

Coerr, Eleanor. *Chang's Paper Pony.* Harper & Row, 1988.

de Paola, Tomie. *The Lady of Guadalupe.* Holiday House, 1980.

———. *The Legend of Bluebonnet.* Putnam, 1983.

Desbarats, Peter. *Gabrielle and Selena*. Harcourt, Brace Jovanovich, 1968.

Esbensen, Barbara Juster. *Ladder to the Sky*. Little, Brown, 1989.

———. *The Star Maiden*. Little, Brown, 1988.

Ets, Marie Hall. *Nine Days to Christmas*. Viking, 1959.

Feelings, Muriel. *Jambo Means Hello: Swahili Alphabet Book*. Dial, 1974.

———. *Moja Means One: Swahali Counting Book*. Dial, 1971.

Flournoy, Valeria. *The Patchwork Quilt*. Dial, 1985.

Friedman, Ina. *How My Parents Learned to Eat*. Houghton Mifflin, 1984.

Fufka, Karama. *My Daddy Is a Cool Dude*. Dial, 1975.

Garcia, Richard. *My Aunt Otilia's Spirits*. Children's Press, 1987.

Goble, Paul. *Beyond the Ridge*. Bradbury, 1989.

———. *Buffalo Woman*. Bradbury, 1984.

———. *Death of the Iron Horse*. Bradbury, 1987.

———. *The Gift of the Sacred Dog*. Bradbury, 1980.

———. *The Girl Who Loved Wild Horses*. Bradbury, 1978.

———. *Iktomi and the Berries*. Watts, 1989.

———. *Iktomi and the Boulder*. Orchard, 1988.

Greenfield, Eloise. *Grandpa's Face*. Philomel, 1988.

———. *Nathaniel Talking*. Black Butterfly Children's Books, 1989.

———. *She Come Bringing Me That Little Baby Girl*. Lippincott, 1974.

Griego, Margot. *Tortillitas Para Mama and Other Spanish Nursery Rhymes*. Holt, Rinehart & Winston, 1981.

Grifalconi, Ann. *The Village of Round and Square Houses*. Little, 1986.

Guy, Rosa. *Mother Crocodile*. Delacorte, 1981.

Haley, Gail. *A Story, a Story*. Atheneum, 1970.

Hamilton, Virginia. *The Time-Ago Tales of Jahdu*. Macmillan, 1969.

Harris, Joel Chandler. *The Tales of Uncle Remus: The Adventures of Brer Rabbit*. Dial, 1987.

Haseley, Dennis. *The Scared One*. Warne, 1983.

Havill, Juanita. *Jamaica's Find*. Houghton Mifflin, 1986.

Hoffman, Mary. *Amazing Grace*. Dial, 1991.

Howard, Elizabeth. *Chita's Christmas Tree*. Bradbury, 1989.

Hyun, Peter. *Korea's Favorite Tales and Lyrics*. Tuttle, 1986.

Ikeda, Daisaku. *Over the Deep Blue Sea*. Knopf, 1992.

Isadora, Rachel. *Ben's Trumpet*. Greenwillow, 1979.

Ishii, Momoko. *The Tongue-Cut Sparrow*. Dutton, 1987.

Jassem, Kate. *Sacajawea, Wilderness Guide*. Troll, 1979.

Johnson, Angela. *Tell Me a Story, Mama*. Watts, 1989.

Keats, Ezra Jack. *Goggles*. Macmillan, 1969.

———. *John Henry, An American Legend*. Pantheon, 1965.

———. *Whistle for Willie*. Viking, 1964.

———. *Pet Show*. Macmillan, 1987.

Kimmel, Eric. *Hershel and the Hanukkah Goblins*. Holiday House, 1989.

Knutson, Barbara, *Why the Crab Has No Head*. Carolrhoda. 1987.

Langstaff, John. *What a Morning!* McEdlerry, 1987.

Lattimore, Deborah. *Flame of Peace: A Tale of the Aztecs*. Harper & Row, 1987.

Leaf, Munro. *Story of Ferdinand*. Viking, 1936.

Lenski, Lois. *Sing a Song of People*. Little, Brown, 1987.

Lester, Julius. *How Many Spots Does a Leopard Have?* Scholastic, 1989.

Levin, Ellen. *I Hate English!* Scholastic, 1989.

Lewin, Hugh. *Jafta*. Carolrhoda, 1983.

————. *Jafta and the Wedding*. Carolrhoda, 1983.

————. *Jafta's Father*. Carolrhoda, 1983.

————. *Jafta's Mother*. Carolrhoda, 1983.

Little, Lessie Jones. *Children of Long Ago*. Philomel, 1988.

Luenn, Nancy. *Nessa's Fish*. Atheneum, 1990.

Lyon, George Ella. *Dreamplace*. Orchard, 1993.

MacLachlan, Patricia. *Through Grandpa's Eyes*. Harper, 1979.

Martel, Cruz. *Yagua Days*. Dial, 1976.

Martin, Bill. *Knots on a Counting Rope*. Holt, Rinehart & Winston, 1987.

Martin, Rafe. *The Rough-Face Girl*. Putnam, 1992.

McDermott, Gerald. *Anasi the Spider*. Holt, 1972.

McKissack, Patricia. *Flossie & the Fox*. Dial, 1986.

————. *A Million of Fish...More or Less*. Knopf, 1992.

————. *Mirandy and Brother Wind*. Knopf, 1988.

————. *Nettie Jo's Friends*. Knopf, 1989.

Mendez, Phil. *The Black Snowman*. Scholastic, 1989.

Miska Miles. *Annie and the Old One*. Little, Brown, 1971.

Monjo, N. *Drinking Gourd*. Harper & Row, 1970.

Mosel, Arlene. *The Funny Little Woman*. Dutton, 1972

Orr, Katherine. *My Grandpa and the Sea*. Carolrhoda, 1990.

Osofsky, Audrey. *Dreamcatcher*. Orchard, 1992.

Politi, Leo. *The Nicest Gift*. Scribner, 1973.

————. *Song of the Swallows*. Scribner 1949.

Pomerantz, Charlotte. *If I Had a Paka*. Greenwillow, 1993.

Prusski, Jeffrey. *Bring Back the Deer*. Harcourt Brace Jovanovich, 1988.

Ringgold, Faith. *Aunt Harriet's Underground Railroad in the Sky*. Crown, 1992.

————. *Tar Beach*. Crown, 1991.

Robbins, Ruth. *How the First Rainbow Was Made*. Parnassus, 1980.

Rutland, Jonathan. *Take a Trip to Spain*. Watts, 1980.

Rylant, Cynthia. *When I Was Young in the Mountains*. Dutton, 1982.

San Souci, Robert D. *Sukey and the Mermaid*. Macmillan, 1992.

————. *The Lost Lake*. Houghton Mifflin, 1989.

Say, Allen. *Tree of Cranes*. Houghton Mifflin, 1991.

Sneve, Virginia. *Jimmy Yellow Hawk*. Holiday House, 1972.

Spencer, Paula Underwood. *Who Speaks for Wolf*. Tribe of Two Press, 1983.

Stanley, Diane. *Shaka: King of the Zulus*. Morrow, 1988.

Steptoe, John. *Daddy is a Monster...Sometimes*. Lippincott, 1980.

————. *Mufaro's Beautiful Daughters*. Lee & Shepard, 1987.

————. *Stevie*. Harper, 1969.

————. *The Story of Jumping Mouse*. Lothrop Lee & Shepard, 1984.

Stevenson, Robert Louis. *My Shadow*. Putnam, 1990.

Stolz, Mary. *Storm in the Night*. Harper, 1988.

Stow, Jenny. *The House that Jack Built*. Dial, 1992.

Surat, Michele Maria. *Angel Child, Dragon Child*. Carnival/Raintree, 1983.

Tobias, Toby. *Arthur Mitchell*. Crowell, 1975.

Toye, William. *The Loon's Necklace*. Oxford, 1977.

Wallas, James. *Kwakiutl Legends*. Hancock House, 1981.

Walter, Mildred Pitts. *Two and Too Much*. Bradbury, 1990.

————. *Ty's One-man Band*. Macmillan, 1980.

Ward, Leila. *I Am Eyes*. Greenwillow, 1978.

White Deer of Autumn. *Ceremony—In the Circle of Life*. Raintree, 1983.

Williams, Karen Lynn. *Galimoto*. Lothrop, Lee & Shepard, 1990.

————. *When Africa Was Home*. Orchard, 1991.

Williams, Vera. *Cherries and Cherry Pits*. Greenwillow, 1986.

Yashima, Taro. *Umbrella*. Viking, 1958.

Young, Ed. *Lon Po Po*. Philomel, 1989.